VIOLENCE
AT
SPORTS EVENTS

BRIAN WINGATE

ROSEN
PUBLISHING®

New York

To Kate

Published in 2009 by The Rosen Publishing Group, Inc.
29 East 21st Street, New York, NY 10010

Library of Congress Cataloging-in-Publication Data

Wingate, Brian.
Violence at Sports Events / Brian Wingate
    p.cm.—(Violence and society)
Includes bibliographical references and index.
ISBN-13: 978-1-4042-1796-6 (library binding)
1. Violence in sports—Juvenile literature. I. Title.
GV706.7.W56 2008
796—dc22

                      2007048351

Manufactured in Malaysia

On the cover: Left: A fan taunts the opposition. Center: Security officials at U.S. Cellular Field in Chicago remove a fan after he attacked an umpire during an April 15, 2003, Chicago White Sox game.

CONTENTS

INTRODUCTION

Official Tommy Nunez Jr. struggles to separate Ben Wallace *(wearing white armband)* of the Detroit Pistons and Ron Artest of the Indiana Pacers. The brawl that ensued resulted in the heaviest fines and longest game suspensions in NBA history.

The night of November 19, 2004, began like many other nights at the Palace, a sports arena in Detroit, Michigan. Fans filled the seats for a basketball game between the home team, the Pistons, and their conference rivals, the Indiana Pacers. The Pacers and the Pistons battled it out that night, and by the end of the game, tempers were running hot. With only minutes remaining in the game, Pistons center Ben Wallace drove to the basket. Pacers player Ron Artest reached over and swiped at the ball, slamming Wallace in the arm and chest. Referee Tommy Nuñez Jr. blew his whistle to signal a foul. Wallace, outraged at such a physical foul, charged Artest and pushed him in the chest. Players from both teams immediately swarmed the court.

In the heat of competition, tempers often flare between players in the playing arena. Usually, fans watch from the sidelines as order is restored and the game resumes. But no one was prepared for what happened next that night at the Palace.

Artest separated himself from the brawl and lay down on the scorer's table at the side of the court. He lounged on his back, arms crossed behind his head, while players jostled and shoved only yards away. Perhaps an angry Pistons fan thought Artest looked like an easy target. A plastic cup filled with ice flew from the stands and struck Artest. Videotape of the incident shows Artest springing into the stands with

fists flying at the person who he thought threw the cup. Teammate Stephen Jackson followed Artest and began throwing punches at fans nearby. Fans, in turn, swung wildly at the players, trying to land a punch. The melee lasted five minutes. As the Pacers' players were finally escorted out through the players' tunnel, they shielded themselves from drink cups, ice, and even folding chairs hurled by the angry crowd.

Deadly Rage

Sports violence is not always carried out by angry mobs. Thomas Junta of Massachusetts is spending six to ten years in state prison for his actions at a pickup ice hockey game. One day in 2000, Junta and his son were playing at a local hockey rink with some other adults and children. Michael Costin was also there with his three sons and was serving as the unofficial referee. According to eyewitnesses, Thomas Junta became upset and protested several rough plays that Costin chose to ignore. Costin shrugged off Junta's concerns, replying that rough play is a part of the sport. Perhaps this snub stoked Junta's rage. Clearly, Junta felt he had a score to settle with Michael Costin, as the men got into two fights after the game. During the second fight, Thomas Junta sat on top of Costin and beat him in the head, killing him.

Crossing the Line

These events are unique because they cross the line between spectator and participant. They also blur the line between the heated battle of competitive sports and unrestrained physical violence. Many sports have violent aspects, and the pressures of

competition can spark conflicts that quickly escalate into on-field confrontations. Pressure is experienced by the players on the court or the field of play, but those who watch the games also feel the highs and lows of the competition they are witnessing. Sometimes, the passions of the moment ignite a situation that suddenly rages out of control. How does the intensity of an athletic contest become a fistfight in the stands, a riot in the streets, or even an excuse for murder?

The events at the Palace involving the Pistons and the Pacers took place on national satellite television. But violence associated with sports events is not always so obvious and open. Every week in local communities across the United States, fans and parents on the sidelines take out their frustrations on referees and players—even their own children.

News stories often say that "sports rage" is on the rise in the world today. Is it true? We will examine some of the pressures experienced by players, fans, and parents at every level of organized sports. We will see how these pressures can lead to unwanted rage and violence. Then we will discuss ways to return to the heart and true gift of the sports we play—the joy of the game itself.

CHAPTER ONE

From Then to Now

There is a good reason that people have played sports for thousands of years. At a very basic level, sports are immensely helpful for our bodies and minds. Sports provide an avenue for vigorous physical exercise and an opportunity to test our physical and mental limits. Team sports foster our ability to work together with others of varying abilities toward a common end. Together, team members learn firsthand how to overcome adversity and reach lofty goals. In short, sports teach us many lessons that we can use regularly throughout our lives.

Many popular sports involve physical contact, so they may also serve as powerful outlets for aggression. The rules of sports are designed to channel players' aggression in productive ways and to maintain certain standards of conduct on the field. But the rules and regulations that manage the aggression on the court or field do not apply to an irate spectator or an angry crowd.

Watching the Action

For many sports events, the players on the field are surrounded by the "other" participants—the spectators. These people who watch the action together come from all walks of life. They have different social backgrounds, ethnic origins, and economic status. But they all share one thing in common: they love the teams they root for. For some, this love can

Screaming fans show their passion and excitement during a game between the University of Miami and their in-state rivals from the University of Florida.

become an unhealthy passion, or obsession. These spectators may become so seized by their emotions that they lose control and disrupt the game itself.

In Europe, the issue of unruly fans and spectator violence usually calls to mind the antisocial behavior of football (soccer) fans. The so-called hooligans of English football are particularly well known, but they are not alone. A recent study shows that about 10 percent of all European matches today are marred by

"serious incidents" involving fan violence. One of the worst incidents of football hooliganism occurred in Brussels in 1985, at the European Cup tournament game between Liverpool and Juventus, an Italian team. Prior to the game, frenzied Liverpool fans charged toward the Italian fan section, causing a retaining wall to collapse. Thirty-nine spectators were killed, and hundreds were injured. Following the disaster, English teams were barred from European Cup games for five years.

Bloodlust—Ancient Roots

Going back in history, we see many examples of athletic contests in which the line separating participant and spectator became blurred. The games and spectacles of the Roman Empire are legendary for their brutality and the bloodlust of the rowdy crowd. Roman historian and philosopher Seneca wrote, "In the morning, they throw men to the lions and bears; at noon, they throw them to the spectators." Prisoners and slaves were trained as expert fighters, or gladiators, who fought each other in the center of the Roman Coliseum before a crowd that included the emperor. Gladiators fought to the death, but the winner would look to the emperor before striking the killing blow. The emperor, in turn, asked the crowd whether the loser should live or die. A hand in the air meant the loser should be spared and given a chance to fight another day. A thumbs-down gesture called for his death. Thousands of gladiators died after receiving a thumbs-down vote from the spectators.

The Mayans of Mexico and Central America were another culture that took athletic contests very seriously. Played as early as 3000 BCE, the Mayan contest called Pok-a-Tok was seen as a symbolic battle between the forces of good and evil. The contest

As the Roman emperor observes from his box, spectators give a victorious gladiator the thumbs-down gesture. By doing this, they demanded the death of his vanquished foe.

almost always ended in death. Accounts differ on the outcome of these contests. Some claim that the captain of the winning team would offer himself to the captain of the losing team to be beheaded. His death thus sent him on a quick path to the heavens, a seat with the gods, and a blessing for his people. Others claim that the losing captain was decapitated. Either way, the contest ended with a brutally violent act in which all spectators were symbolic participants.

The Past and the Present

Sports still carry the thrill of violence and confrontation that fueled sporting events thousands of years ago. For example, today's mixed martial artists pummel each other into bloody submission on pay-per-view television, a sight reminiscent of the ancient Roman gladiators. Or, as another example, massive football players race around the field at full speed, looking to deliver bone-rattling hits to players on the opposite team. These modern sports are heavily regulated to preserve the intensity of competition without needless violence. Commissions (governing bodies) set strict rules and guidelines for both players and fans, and commissioners determine fines and suspensions for anyone who breaks the rules.

But the rules have not totally erased the past. Crowds still long to see their favorite players and teams vanquish their foes. In many cases, simple violence is still celebrated, especially in the sports and news media. During the football season, for example, ESPN showcases the biggest hits of the weekend on a segment called "Jacked Up." NASCAR highlights usually feature every fender-bender and fiery crash. Hockey recaps show opposing players squaring off with fists flying. These highlight shows cannot convey the flow of an entire game, so they must boil down a three-hour contest to a one-minute reel that spotlights only a few things. We celebrate the winners and sometimes belittle the losers. We watch the most brilliant plays and most violent moments, often in slow motion. The rhythm and flow of the game itself is lost. Players take this mentality onto the field: make an impact and win at all costs.

Nothing New

In 2004, the Associated Press published an article called "Ugly Sports Incidents Nothing New," which recounted violence involving fans and/or players dating back more than a hundred years. Notable events described in the article include:

- July 11, 1886—A beer mug thrown from the stands strikes umpire George Bradley in the sixth inning of a baseball game.
- October 9, 1934—Fans throw tomatoes at St. Louis Cardinals player Joe Medwick in Game 7 of the World Series.
- December 23, 1979—Boston Bruins player Stan Jonathan and several teammates brawl with fans in the stands, after Jonathan is hit in the face with a flying object. Teammate Mike Millbury removes one fan's shoe and beats him with it.
- August 27, 1986—Wally Joyner, first baseman for the California Angels, is hit in the arm by a knife thrown from the stands of Yankee Stadium. He is unhurt.
- December 23, 1995—Snowball-throwing fans disrupt an NFL game between the San Diego Chargers and New York Giants, knocking San Diego's equipment manager unconscious.
- September 19, 2002—A father and son jump from the stands and attack Kansas City Royals first-base coach Tom Gamboa during a game at Comiskey Park. They grab him from behind, throw him to the ground, and begin punching and kicking him. Both attackers are arrested and charged with aggravated battery (a felony).

Big Sports Equals Big Business

The gladiator battles in the Roman Empire were phenomenally popular. In 264 BCE, the first contest pitted three pairs of slaves against each other. By 145 BCE, ninety pairs of slaves raged for three days. The battles proved to be so popular that, eventually, there were gladiatorial fights of some sort going on at all times.

Modern football stadiums like the Dallas Cowboys' Texas Stadium *(above)* **recall the Roman Coliseum, where thousands of spectators cheered for both displays of violence and skill.**

The Coliseum, perhaps the world's most famous arena, was completed in 80 CE by the emperor Titus. It held 385,000 people, dwarfing today's stadiums. For comparison, the average NFL stadium can seat 68,000 fans.

The spectacle of sports is a proven moneymaker, and the business of professional sports has never been bigger. Harvard professor Paul Weiler studied the growth of professional sports over the last fifty years. Weiler's research results are discussed in "The Dow of Professional Sports," an article written by Craig Lambert. Weiler observed that the value of the Dow Jones Industrial Average, which measures the value of corporate America, is twenty times greater than in 1960. In contrast, the value of the National Football League (NFL) has multiplied more than seven hundred times in the same period. The Dallas Cowboys cost $600,000 to establish in 1960. By 1998, the team was valued at $1 billion.

Players have certainly benefited from this flow of cash. Weiler found that by the 1990s, the average professional athlete earned more than thirty-five times the average amount earned in 1974. High draft picks in major sports are now paid millions in signing bonuses before they even step foot in the professional arena.

Shadow Side

When young athletes see these wealthy stars as role models, it can be easy to lose the heart of the sport and focus only on individual achievement. Rather than focusing on their own best efforts, some players will do just about anything to win. This is an aspect of athletic competition we try not to focus on—the "shadow side" of sports. It is at the heart of many incidents of violence at sports events.

W hen news outlets report on violent outbreaks related to sports events these days, it seems they are focused on incidents involving the fans and parents as often as the competitors. These events are not unique to North America. Violence at sporting events is a global issue. Consider some of these recent events:

- In Argentina, twenty-nine people were killed at football (soccer) matches during the 1990s.
- In April 2006, at Nehru Stadium in India, police fired tear gas into a crowd of twenty thousand fans who threw stones and burned posters after a cricket match was cancelled.
- In 2006, Greek lawmakers promised to toughen laws that will result in jail time for violent fans at sporting events.
- In November 2007, a soccer fan in Rome, Italy, was accidentally shot and killed by a police officer attempting to break up a fight between fans of rival teams. Hundreds of angry fans attacked the police station and broke windows at the Italian Olympic Committee headquarters located nearby.

News stories like these have caused many to claim that violence at sports events—also called sports rage or sideline

Fans of rival teams clash at a soccer match in Rome in November 2007. This skirmish ended with the accidental shooting death of a fan by an Italian policeman.

rage—is a growing epidemic in North America and abroad. This may be true, but so far there is little scientific evidence to back up this claim. Is sports rage really on the rise? Gregg Heinzmann, director of the Youth Sports Research Council, doesn't think so. In his article "Parental Violence in Youth Sports," he states that only one scientific study has been conducted on the issue of sports rage. In his opinion, "there is currently no scientific evidence to substantiate the claim

that violence in youth sports is 'escalating' or 'out of control.'"
Heinzmann may be right, but there is no doubt that violence
in sports is an issue that needs to be addressed.

Blanket Coverage

Media coverage has completely changed the nature of sports in
world culture. It's hard to believe, but as recently as fifty years
ago, in order to see a game, you had to be present in the stadium
or arena. You might have been able to catch a baseball game on
the radio, but live television broadcasts of sports events were
expensive to produce and therefore rare. Before long, however,
technology improved. With the inventions of satellite and cable
television service, live sports broadcasts became much more
common. Today, every major sport has television coverage at
every game. A typical football fan follows several games on
Sunday just by flipping the channel on the remote control.
The Super Bowl is broadcast to hundreds of millions of homes
across the globe. In this way, professional sports have become
a global media property—and a high-value commodity.

The rise of the Internet has taken sports and spectator access
to yet another level. We now have a twenty-four-hour news cycle
in a connected world that never truly sleeps. News outlets
are on the hunt around the clock to get the latest and most
provocative breaking news. So, if an irate parent attacks a coach
in California on Tuesday night, you'll know about it in Florida
before Wednesday morning. Violence catches our attention, and
little goes unreported.

It may be hard to prove whether violent incidents are
increasing, but the subject has grabbed worldwide attention,

and most organized sports are moving quickly to stamp out violent behavior. We will examine their strategies in chapter 4.

What Causes the Pressure to Build?

No matter how well they are regulated, sports will remain a pressure-filled environment for many reasons. The sheer

Excited fans form a sea of yellow at an Arizona State University Sun Devils football game. The wild cheering of spectators can ratchet up the intensity of the game on the field.

intensity of sporting events provides much of the allure for players and fans alike. When kept in proper perspective, the pressure of sports can be thrilling and rewarding. But when perspective is lost, things can fly out of control. To understand how this happens, one can examine some of the factors involved in a typical game on the professional or amateur level.

Athletes and Coaches

On the professional level, athletes and coaches are paid hand-somely to perform at a high level. As a result, they are under a great deal of pressure to produce results. Those who do not perform well are often referred to as being in the "hot seat" and in danger of being pulled from the action altogether. Coaches in all professional sports are routinely fired when their teams fail to produce wins. Take the example of longtime New York Yankees manager Joe Torre. He won four World Series pennants in twelve years with the team, yet when his contract expired in 2007, the Yankees offered him a one-year deal with a reduction in his salary. Torre refused, calling the offer an insult. It was widely believed that the Yankees did not want Torre to return because he had failed to guide the team back to the World Series in the previous three years.

Referees and Umpires

Referees are supposed to be fair and impartial judges of the game. But even the best referee makes a bad call once in a while. If the bad call is crucial to the fate of one of the teams, then players, coaches, and fans can quickly get overheated. Professional sports arenas have the luxury of having security officers to protect

With the Internet, professional as well as amateur footage of sports violence can be seen worldwide within minutes. Here, an angry father charges a youth league referee in this clip on YouTube (www.youtube.com).

referees and umpires from unruly fans, but youth and high school leagues do not. Many sports officials report being cursed at and spat upon by angry parents. Some now purchase assault insurance in case they are attacked and injured. At least eleven states have passed laws prohibiting the assault of referees or umpires.

A survey by the National Association of Sports Officials (NASO) found that 76 percent of the respondents from sixty high

school athletic associations reported that "increased spectator interference" has caused many officials to quit. NASO president Barry Mano believes violence toward sports officials is a serious problem. "We get reports here every single week of an assault against a sports official on some level," Mano said in a 2007 interview with the *Stockton Record*. "The problem . . . has been getting worse over the last five years."

Fans and Media Coverage

The word "fan" is short for "fanatic," meaning one who is excessively enthusiastic in his or her devotion to something. Some fans are more relaxed about their involvement in the game, but others pour a great deal of time, money, and energy into supporting their favorite team. For these fans, the pressures of athletic competition can fuel passions to a dangerous degree.

As media coverage has increased in professional sports, the spotlight has extended beyond the playing field. Players are now superstars in their own right. They are not only athletes but entertainers as well. And the biggest stars are held under constant scrutiny by the media. Fans can follow the lives of their favorite players like never before with the rise of Internet pages, blogs, and twenty-four-hour sports channels. Fans identify themselves with their favorite team or player, and, as a result, they are deeply involved on an emotional level.

The sources of frustration when watching a favorite team are almost endless. Botched plays, poor officiating, lackluster performances, subpar playing conditions, and the behavior of opposing fans are just a few of the factors that can stoke the intensity level at any game.

In 1995, this man became the poster boy for boorish fan behavior when he was photographed hurling a snowball onto the field at an NFL game between the New York Giants and the San Diego Chargers. Giants officials offered a reward for his identity, and the man was later arrested.

Fans and Vicarious Power

Following a team can be a way for the spectator to escape the stresses of daily life. In these cases, the success of the team is thought to reflect personally upon individual fans. Sometimes, entire cities identify closely with their hometown teams. For example, in November 2007, Jemele Hill wrote a feature article on ESPN.com about Jon Kitna, quarterback for the Detroit Lions. In the article, Hill wrote about the importance of the football team in keeping up the spirits of the town: "The local papers are smattered with news of high foreclosure rates and auto plant layoffs, but if you check the most-viewed stories on either the *Detroit News'* or *Detroit Free Press'* Web sites, a Lions story will almost certainly be the most popular, well ahead of whatever economic doom is forecasted for the day."

Rabid fans can have a distorted perception of their own involvement in the action on the field. In Wilbert Leonard's *A Sociological Perspective of Sport*, sociologist Irving Goldaber says, "When people come into the stands, they begin to feel the power to affect the outcome of the game. Now there is a feeling they can do something to help." When this attitude is combined with highly charged emotions and pride, Goldaber says, sports are opened up to a new trend in fan violence.

One indicator of this trend is the rising rate of post-game riots in cities and at colleges across the United States. It is increasingly common for victorious fans to take to the streets and damage public property in a rowdy celebration. Kent State University sociologist Jerry Lewis estimates that there are ten to fifteen such large-scale riots after sporting events each year. In these events, fans act as though they have won the contest

Celebration turns to riot, as frenzied fans overturn a car in the streets of Columbus, Ohio, in 2002. Their Ohio State football team had just defeated rival Michigan.

themselves, and feelings of pride and superiority overcome common sense. In Chicago, for example, fans raged through the city after the Chicago Bulls won the 1992 NBA championship, inflicting more than $10 million in damages. One thousand people were arrested in the delirious victory "celebration."

Rivalries

Most sports have long traditions of rivalries that are played out over years or even decades. These rivalries develop between teams at all levels, from local Little Leagues to the global stage. In international soccer events, such as the World Cup tournament, teams carry the hopes of entire nations on their shoulders. Sometimes, the teams on the field represent nations that have a history of conflict or war. When this is the case, the tension on the field and in the stands can be very high. Some sociologists point to this dynamic as the cause of much of the spectator violence that mars international soccer matches involving teams from Germany, Italy, and England.

School teams, too, are known for their heated rivalries. When their team wins, student fans usually celebrate and take delight in taunting students supporting the losing team. Such team rivalries are often regional, with opposing teams from the same geographical area battling for supremacy year after year. For example, the University of North Carolina at Chapel Hill and Duke University are only eleven miles (seventeen kilometers) apart in the heart of North Carolina. Their rivalry is considered the fiercest in college basketball, and entire books have been written about the subject. With students tormenting the opposing school with a feeling that verges on hatred, it's easy to see how such an emotional environment could spark a violent outbreak.

Escalating Behaviors

Especially in a college or professional setting, yelling at the action is an expected and enjoyable part of the experience. There is

Mere feet from the action on the floor, Duke students taunt a player from archrival UNC-Chapel Hill, as she inbounds the basketball.

nothing quite like the thrill of twenty thousand people jumping to their feet in excitement at the same time. But trouble brews when spectator behavior loses the spirit of the game and becomes personal. It is normal for a fan to groan in disgust when a call goes against his or her team. But the line is crossed when the fan harasses the referee for the remainder of the game and interferes with his or her ability to perform effectively. Sometimes, fans will

turn and taunt someone who is supporting the opposing team. Taunting takes the shared experience of the crowd and turns it into a personal attack. When people feel attacked, they can fell enraged and retaliate. Soon, a brawl can erupt.

The mob mentality, or herd mentality, is another factor that plays a role in escalating fan behavior. Being part of a crowd can make an individual lose a sense of responsibility for his or her actions. In this mind-set, people in a group may do things that they would never do if they were acting individually—like assaulting someone verbally or physically.

Dangerous Brew

Combine these factors, add alcohol, and stir. That is the recipe for a disaster. Beer is sold at most professional sports venues, usually in generous-sized containers. Engrossed in the action, some fans guzzle beers without realizing how much they have had to drink. Too much alcohol causes people to lose their inhibitions—the inner voices that tell all of us to keep our base emotions and hungers in check. With impaired judgment and excited emotions, spectators can easily get carried away.

CHAPTER THREE

Parental Pressure

When Thomas Junta attacked Michael Costin at the ice hockey rink in 2000 (see Introduction, page 6), many people were shocked that one parent could physically assault another while children stood by and watched it happen. Unfortunately, it was not an isolated incident. Sports expert Dennis Docheff recounts several other chilling cases of parents losing control in his article "It's No Longer a Spectator Sport." In May 2003, Docheff writes, "a Little League secretary in Wakefield, Massachusetts, faced criminal charges of assault and battery for allegedly kicking and swearing at an eleven-year-old boy who had been fighting with her son at the baseball field. In September 2003, a Toronto father was charged with assault after grabbing and shaking his ten-year-old daughter's face mask at a youth hockey game."

Amateur and youth sports have a different type of dangerous fan: the over-involved parent. Parenting and sports can be a volatile mixture. Most parents are their child's number-one fans. The thrill of sports comes not just from the action on the field but also from the joy of watching their child perform. As a result, they are often deeply invested in the outcome. When they see their child losing on the field, some parents are unable to control their emotional reactions. If a parent has high hopes and dreams for his or her child, sports can be agonizing. This emotional roller coaster is sometimes too much to bear, and the parent behaves inappropriately.

Joy and pride warm this mother's face as she cheers for her child at a peewee hockey game. Parents typically feel a wide range of emotions when watching their children perform.

In this chapter, we will look at some of the pressures experienced by the parents of young athletes and how these can lead to physical and verbal violence on the sidelines.

Living Vicariously Through the Child

Parents often see their children as a reflection or an extension of themselves, and this dynamic may extend to the sports field. If parents played sports when they were younger, they may try to relive their own glory days through the accomplishments of their children. Such parents unconsciously place extra pressure on their children to succeed. Then the parents may be unreasonably disappointed or angry if their children do not perform up to expectations.

Family Expectations

Sometimes, a sport is passed down from parent to child, and it becomes part of the family tradition. A mother who was a successful swimmer may enroll her five-year-old daughter in swim classes. It may be expected that all the children in the family will be swimmers. This is fine—as long as the children enjoy it. But the subtle pressures of expectation can weigh heavily on children who do not share the same passion for the sport. They may secretly wish they could stop playing altogether but are unable to voice their true feelings.

"What will the neighbors think?" is what some parents are worrying as they watch their child compete. These parents feel that their child's performance on the field is a direct reflection of their worth as parents and their childrearing skills in general.

This is a dangerous dynamic because a child cannot be expected to carry the burden of preserving the image of the family.

Unrealistic Dreams of Success

All parents dream of a bright future for their children. And with a global culture that lavishes rewards on its athletic stars, sports

Proud parents congratulate their son for winning a sports trophy. Children thrive when parents are supportive but do not have unrealistic goals for them.

can appear to parents as a golden ticket to their child's happiness and financial prosperity. Some children show great promise in a sport from a very young age, distinguishing themselves from their teammates through innate talent and coordination. Parents of these children may be fooled into thinking that their child is headed for athletic stardom at the very highest levels. The chances that this will happen, however, are very slim.

The Cost of Greatness

Grooming a child for athletic stardom can be a huge financial investment. In his article "How to Raise a Tour Pro," Josh Sens interviewed Mac Thayer, the executive director of the Junior Golf Scoreboard. Thayer estimates that parents can expect to spend up to $20,000 per year on travel costs, private instruction, and tournament expenses for top junior golfers. With so much money invested in their children, parents can easily feel entitled to a return on their money. This will almost certainly increase the sense of disappointment and frustration if their child fails to perform.

Higher Education, Higher Costs

Few parents are able to spend $20,000 on sports fees every year. In fact, most parents face more practical concerns—financing their child's education, for instance. The cost of a college education is very high. Fortunately for some outstanding athletes, many colleges and universities provide a limited number of scholarships for their student-athletes. A full athletic scholarship, or "full ride," pays for all tuition costs and many other school-related expenses. As a result, competition for scholarships is fierce.

For a handful of stellar high school athletes in many different sports, the costs of higher education are paid for by full athletic scholarships.

Even for the parents of excellent athletes, the chances that their child will receive an athletic scholarship are not good. The National Collegiate Athletic Association (NCAA) reports that only about 3 percent of the four million high school athletes in the United States will receive full or partial athletic scholarships to attend college. Still, to an anxious parent on the sidelines, a bad game played in front of college scouts can symbolize the loss of college tuition for the next four years.

An online advertisement for the Phil Adams Athletic Scholarship Concierge Service illustrates how sports recruiting has become a big business. The owners of the service promise to save "between $23,000–$45,000 in annual college tuition costs." They promise that "utilizing an elite athletic scholarship service during the recruiting process will give your son or daughter a definite advantage."

Win-at-All-Cost Attitude

If parents are engaging in sports activities with any of the issues discussed here, they are more likely to adopt a win-at-all-cost attitude. If this happens, they just have too much riding on the fortunes of their child. Legendary Green Bay Packers coach Vince Lombardi said, "Winning isn't everything; it's the only thing." Similarly, Oakland Raiders owner Al Davis is famous for telling his players and coaches, "Just win, baby." At the professional level, where people's livelihoods depend on the outcome of a game, it's easy to see why players, coaches, and owners think winning is "the only thing." And when the pressure to win is ratcheted up so high, it shouldn't be a big surprise when the physical battles on the field spill over into violence in the stands.

The Saga of Mary Pierce

When Mary Pierce first started playing tennis at age ten, she probably had no idea that within six years she would be a highly ranked competitor on the world stage. But one person certainly knew it could happen. Mary's father, Jim Pierce, quit his job as a jeweler to coach Mary full-time. By age sixteen, his daughter was a rising force on the women's tennis circuit and a worthy opponent.

Players respected Mary's prowess on the court, but no one could say the same for Jim's behavior. An outspoken and unyielding man, Jim drove Mary to succeed with an unrelenting regimen of physical training and verbal commands. Tennis crowds were aghast as Jim screamed obscenities at his daughter during matches. He showed no remorse for his tactics, typically pointing to her success as justification for his approach. In an interview with the *Sporting News*, Jim described his grueling methods: "For seven years, eight hours a day, I hit 700 serves at Mary. We used to work until midnight. My young son slept by the net. I wouldn't let Mary leave until she got it right. Sure, she cried. I cried too. So what?" Jim Pierce seemed to revel in his position as star maker and tyrant trainer. After a match in August 1991, the *New York Times* reported him as saying, "To put up with me and everything else, she's got to be like God, mentally. She hasn't gotten a single call in two years because everyone hates me."

After eight years, Mary Pierce decided she had had enough. In July 1993, she announced that she was relieving Jim of his coaching duties. At a news conference in New Jersey, Mary remarked, "We'll still keep our relationship, we'll be together. As far as tennis is concerned, we were just fighting a lot." A week later she filed a legal restraining order to prevent Jim from attending her matches.

Jim Pierce applauds at one of his daughter Mary's tennis matches in this 1990 photo. Three years later, his overbearing behavior led Mary to fire him as her coach.

This, however, is a terrible model for youth and amateur sports. The "winning is everything" attitude quickly drains the joy out of the game for young players.

When young people play sports, they are still in a world run by adults, so the attitude and behavior of the adults play a huge part in their child's experience of sports. If the adults' attitude

The Green Bay Packers carry their coach, Vince Lombardi, after winning the Western Division title in 1960. Lombardi's win-at-all-cost attitude worked in the NFL, but it would have made him a lousy youth league coach.

is poor, young players will not enjoy the sport. As evidence, in his article "Pressure Points," Chris Wagner recounts the results of a recent Michigan State Youth Sports Institute survey. The survey lists "adults, particularly parents," as the main cause for kids dropping out of athletics and the primary reason for game playing becoming a "joyless, negative experience."

Finding Perspective

The pressure of winning at all costs distorts our perception of what it means to play the game. Trouble begins when the only thing that matters is the outcome. A coach or parent who just focuses on the final score may overlook the other benefits of organized sports, and overbearing adults can make young players feel as though their best efforts are never enough unless they result in victory. When players, parents, and coaches keep things in perspective, however, it's clear to all that most of the true benefits of sports come from participation in the game itself. Who walks off with a trophy is not nearly as important as the experience that all players gain, even those on the losing team.

CHAPTER FOUR

It's Just a Game—
Finding Solutions

If violence at sports events were indeed dangerously out of control, participation levels would probably be falling. After all, it would make sense for young people to seek out safer and healthier activities. But that doesn't seem to be what is happening. In fact, the popularity of organized youth sports is growing and shows no sign of abating. A survey by the National Federation of State High School Associations reported that student participation in high school athletics for the 2006–2007 school year jumped by the largest amount in ten years. More than 183,000 students began playing high school athletics, bringing the national total to almost 7.5 million participants.

Strategies for Fun

When it comes to sports, kids still know how to have fun. On the amateur level, it seems that the parents and coaches are the ones who need a friendly reminder now and then. Neighborhood leagues and interscholastic organizations across the United States and Canada have realized that merely organizing the games themselves is no longer enough.

Below are some of the strategies being used to keep the focus on fun and avoid the pressures that may lead to violence.

Interscholastic sports continue to thrive in North America. This football game in 2006 between the St. Xavier Tigers and the Trinity Shamrocks in Kentucky continues one of the longest high school rivalries in the United States.

Codes of Conduct

Youth sports organizations have begun laying down firm ground rules for anyone who wishes to participate in sports as a spectator or team member. Many neighborhood sports associations now require parents to sign a conduct agreement form before their child is allowed to enroll in athletic activities. These agreements make clear the expectations for parental involvement and sideline behavior. Consequences for aggressive or disruptive displays are plainly stated. For example, New Jersey's Code of Conduct permits the school board or youth sports team organization to "ban the presence of any person at youth sports events who (1) engages in verbal or physical threats or abuse aimed at any student, coach, official or parent, or (2) initiates a fight or scuffle with any student, coach, official, parent, or other person if the conduct occurs at or in connection with a school- or community-sponsored youth sports event."

Punishment may include game suspensions for the parent or both the parent and child. The sports association is then covered by a clear code of conduct in case it is necessary to remove a parent from the sidelines.

No Scoring

Football coach Vince Lombardi once mused, "If winning isn't everything, why do they keep score?"

In the world of professional sports, keeping score is a necessary part of the game. But a lopsided loss can cause young athletes to get discouraged or embarrassed, making tempers more likely to flare. Especially for younger athletes, playing without

Displays such as this rowdy and aggressive fan attacking another spectator will hopefully become a thing of the past as leagues at every level of sports adopt strict codes of conduct for both fans and players.

keeping score can keep the focus on building skills, developing teamwork, and just having fun. Winning can come later.

Youth soccer leagues have been some of the first to adopt the concept. In the early 1990s, U.S. Youth Soccer recommended that athletes under ten years old should not keep score, have league standings, or receive trophies for winning games. State and national ruling bodies for youth soccer have followed suit with similar advice.

Fancy scoreboards may look strangely blank when leagues adopt no-scoring policies. However, without a score to distract them, it's more likely that young players will focus on the fun of playing the game.

Youth soccer clubs went to a no-scoring system for young players several years ago in Boston, Massachusetts. Coaches and parents found that the children still keep track of the score and do care about whether they win or lose, as it gives them a way to measure their own sense of progress. But by deemphasizing the score, children are encouraged to relax and have fun. Experts note that as soon as you start to formalize the score, the pressure and expectations rise on everyone involved—coaches, parents, and kids.

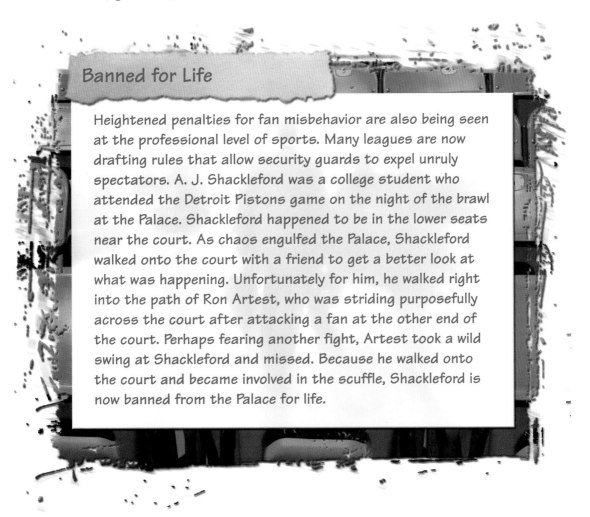

Banned for Life

Heightened penalties for fan misbehavior are also being seen at the professional level of sports. Many leagues are now drafting rules that allow security guards to expel unruly spectators. A. J. Shackleford was a college student who attended the Detroit Pistons game on the night of the brawl at the Palace. Shackleford happened to be in the lower seats near the court. As chaos engulfed the Palace, Shackleford walked onto the court with a friend to get a better look at what was happening. Unfortunately for him, he walked right into the path of Ron Artest, who was striding purposefully across the court after attacking a fan at the other end of the court. Perhaps fearing another fight, Artest took a wild swing at Shackleford and missed. Because he walked onto the court and became involved in the scuffle, Shackleford is now banned from the Palace for life.

Silent Saturdays and Sundays

The roar of the crowd may seem like a necessary ingredient in any sports event, but some neighborhood sports leagues are hoping that a silent crowd will improve the experience for the players. If a team plays every weekend, one game per month may be a silent game. This means the parents must watch the

Parents quietly watch the action at a Little League game in Santa Monica, California. Silent games encourage a more relaxed atmosphere for players and fans alike.

action quietly, or they will be asked to leave. They are allowed to clap their hands to encourage their children, but yelling or dispensing coaching advice from the sideline is forbidden.

The Jack London Soccer Club was one of the largest leagues to go silent when it introduced the approach in October 2004. The league held 7,000 players on 350 teams at the time. C. W. Nevius of SFGate.com covered the transition to silent games in his article "Soccer Players Get the Silent Treatment." He found the response to be overwhelmingly positive. One ten-year-old boy was thrilled to hear that parents would be required to hold their tongues. A mother noticed that, as the game progressed, the children began to communicate and coach themselves on the field. "Either they had a chance to do it because we were quiet," she said, "or they've been doing it all along and we couldn't hear them."

Fan Penalties

Some youth soccer leagues have found a unique way to keep fan behavior in check. In normal play, referees display a yellow card as a warning for extreme on-field fouls, such as bad language or vicious tackles. In some areas now, the crowd, too, can be assigned a yellow card. If one team's fans are unruly, the referee holds up his yellow card and points it toward the sideline. This is the warning card. If the behavior continues, the fans may be given a red card, and their team automatically forfeits the game.

Proactive Prevention

These approaches all provide firm boundaries around the rules of the game, and they serve to protect and preserve the experience

of young athletes. But these punitive measures (punishments) are not the only way to curb violent behaviors. It is also possible to take positive action before the negative action even begins. By following a few simple steps, teams can put the "we" back in team. The following examples are ways to proactively prevent violence from occurring.

Emphasize Relationships

The beginning of the season is the ideal time for a coach to organize a get-together for all the parents and players who are about to embark on the season. This is an opportunity for the coach to establish a relationship with each parent and for parents to meet the other kids on the team. When parents get to know the other kids, they are more likely to root for the team in general instead of only cheering for their own child. A team that socializes away from practices and games develops camaraderie and close relationships that make the team stronger.

Coaches Set the Tone

Coaches play an important part in the lives of young athletes. They are teachers, role models, and even stand-ins for the athletes' parents. Coaches are also authority figures whose behavior is often crucial to maintaining order on the sidelines of recreational league games. A coach who yells at players or throws his or her clipboard when frustrated sets the stage for poor behavior on the sidelines, on the field, and in the stands.

On the other hand, coaches who give and command respect can help to control the behavior of everyone involved in the game. When parents start to lose their cool in the stands,

Parents show their support by lining up for a round of high fives after a game well played. By taking the time to encourage the other children, these parents help to build a more cohesive team.

a coach should take the opportunity to approach the crowd and say, "I know you're here to support your children, but your yelling is disrupting the game. I need you to lower your voice, or you will be asked to leave."

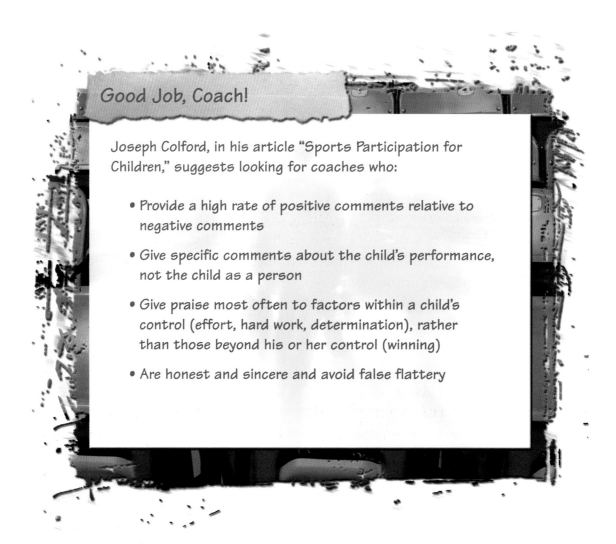

Good Job, Coach!

Joseph Colford, in his article "Sports Participation for Children," suggests looking for coaches who:

- Provide a high rate of positive comments relative to negative comments

- Give specific comments about the child's performance, not the child as a person

- Give praise most often to factors within a child's control (effort, hard work, determination), rather than those beyond his or her control (winning)

- Are honest and sincere and avoid false flattery

Involve the Parents

Many parents need to feel as though they have a voice in their child's sport. A good coach may ask parents for advice on their children's strengths in order to prepare a better game plan. If the parents feel involved and know their feedback is being taken into consideration, they are more likely to relax and enjoy the flow of the game.

Let the Coach Do the Coaching

Once the game begins, it is important for parents to step back and let the coach do the coaching. Some parents are tempted to yell advice throughout the game. General comments are fine, like "Great effort!" This is encouraging to the players. But when a parent tries to critique plays during the game or shout instructions to specific players, his or her advice might conflict with the instructions of the coach. This can be confusing for the athletes and grating to the other parents, and ultimately it helps no one.

Young Athletes Have a Voice

Athletes playing youth sports should always feel that they have a choice and a voice: a choice of whether to play, and a voice to express concerns. An overbearing coach can make life miserable for a team. But there is strength in numbers. Four or five players can ask to speak with their coach and express their concerns. If the coach does not respond, players can talk to an assistant coach or the league directors. If the league is unresponsive, it may even be necessary to switch leagues.

Similarly, children need to feel that they have a voice with their own parents. If your parents' behavior on the sidelines is causing problems, you might seek the help of your coach to let your parents know, kindly but firmly, that they need to step back and quiet down.

Even at high levels of play, many young athletes understand that sports is all about fun and respectful competition. Here, third-place finisher Jon Olsson *(right)* happily congratulates second-place finisher Tanner Hall at a 2005 Winter X Games medal ceremony.

Conclusion

Playing sports is valuable for many reasons. It provides a fun way to test one's limits, both physically and mentally. Athletes also improve their individual skills while learning to play as part of a team. And it is always a thrill to bring one's best effort to the heat of competition against an opposing team or player. The challenge is for athletes, fans, coaches, and parents to maintain the balance between the rush of competition, the thrill of victory, and the emotions of defeat.

As the landscape of sport evolves, we are beginning to see signs of change and the promise that the emphasis is returning to good, clean fun. The X Games provide a great example of individual sports where competitors openly cheer for one another, laugh together during competitions, and express genuine respect for each other. Ryan Slabaugh of the *Vail Daily* newspaper hung out at Winter X Games Nine in 2005. He observed that the X Gamers "are positive, worldly, and know more about hard work and dedication than most adults." Slabaugh observed that Shaun White, the biggest snowboarding star at the games, merely cracked a joke when the judges gave him a lower score than expected. No stomping or swearing, just fun.

And kids are taking notice. A Harris Interactive poll in 2000 found that the X Games were the second-most-appealing sporting event to kids ages six to seventeen, second only to the Olympic Games. Given the choice of violent spectacle or good, clean fun, the kids will choose fun every time.

allure Attraction or temptation.

botch To ruin through clumsiness.

camaraderie Goodwill and lighthearted rapport between or among friends.

concierge Person in charge of special services for clients or guests.

delirious Wild with excitement; enthusiastic.

dynamic Pattern or process of change or activity.

escalate To increase in intensity and scope.

hurtle To rush violently; move with great speed.

impartial Not biased; treating all equally.

innate Existing in one from birth; inborn; native.

irate Extremely angry; enraged.

melee Confused, hand-to-hand fighting in a pitched battle.

muse To consider or say thoughtfully.

prowess Exceptional or superior ability, skill, or strength.

pummel To beat or thrash with or as if with the fists.

restraining order A judicial order to forbid a particular act until a decision is reached.

subpar Not measuring up to traditional standards of performance, value, or production.

tyrant Person in a position of authority who exercises power oppressively or unjustly.

vanquish To overcome in battle; to defeat.

vicarious Felt or enjoyed through imagined participation in the experience of others.

Center for the Study of Sport in Society
360 Huntington Avenue
Richards Hall, Suite 350
Boston, MA 02115
(617) 373-4025
Web site: http://www.sportinsociety.org
The Center for the Study of Sport in Society at Northeastern University is a social justice organization that uses sport to create social change.

National Alliance for Youth Sports (NAYS)
2050 Vista Parkway
West Palm Beach, FL 33411
(800) 688-KIDS (5437)
Web site: http://www.nays.org
The National Alliance for Youth Sports is an advocate for positive and safe sports and activities for children.

National Association of Intercollegiate Athletics (NAIA)
1200 Grand Boulevard
Kansas City, MO 64106
(816) 595-8000
Web site: http://naia.cstv.com
The purpose of the NAIA is to promote the education and development of students through intercollegiate athletic participation.

National Collegiate Athletic Association (NCAA)
6201 College Boulevard
Overland Park, KS 66211
(913) 339-1906
Web site: http://www.ncaa.org
The NCAA governs intercollegiate competition in the United States.

National Federation of State High School Associations (NFHS)
P.O. BOX 690
Indianapolis, IN 46206
(317) 972-6900
Web site: http://www.nfhs.org
The NFHS sets directions for the future by building awareness and support, improving the participation experience, establishing consistent standards and rules for competition, and helping those who oversee high school sports and activities.

Positive Coaching Alliance
3430 West Bayshore Road, Suite 104
Palo Alto, CA 94303
(866) 725-0024
Web site: http://www.positivecoach.org
Positive Coaching Alliance is transforming youth sports so sports can transform youth. It partners with more than 1,100 youth sports organizations, leagues, schools, and cities nationwide.

Web Sites

Due to the changing nature of Internet links, Rosen Publishing has developed an online list of Web sites related to the subject of this book. This site is updated regularly. Please use this link to access the list:

http://www.rosenlinks.com/vas/vase

Aaseng, Nathan. *The Locker Room Mirror: How Sports Reflect Society*. New York, NY: Walker and Company, 1993.

Berger, Gilda. *Violence and Sports*. New York, NY: Franklin Watts, 1990.

Blauner, Andrew, ed. *Coach: 25 Writers Reflect on People Who Made a Difference*. New York, NY: Warner Books, 2005.

Currie, Stephen. *Issues in Sports*. San Diego, CA: Lucent Books, 1998.

Friedman, Steve. *The Agony of Victory: When Winning Isn't Enough*. New York, NY: Arcade, 2007.

Garlett, Kyle, and Patrick O'Neal. *The Worst Call Ever!* New York, NY: Collins, 2007.

Kilmeade, Brian. *It's How You Play the Game: The Powerful Sports Moments That Taught Lasting Values to America's Finest*. New York, NY: Harper Entertainment, 2007.

Margeneau, Eric. *Sports Without Pressure: A Guide for Parents & Coaches of Young Athletes*. New York, NY: Gardner Press, 1990.

BIBLIOGRAPHY

ABC News. "How to Handle Sideline Sports Rage: Parents Behave Badly at Kids' Games." 2005. Retrieved October 21, 2007 (http://abcnews.go.com/GMA/ESPNSports/story?id = 1034449&page = 1).

Asser, Martin. "Analysis: Soccer Violence an International Problem." BBC Online, June 19, 2000. Retrieved November 28, 2007 (http://news.bbc.co.uk/1/hi/world/europe/797601.stm).

August, Roland. *Cruelty and Civilization: The Roman Games.* New York, NY: Routledge, 1998.

Bondy, Filip. "Pierce Rallies as Her Dad Rants and Raves." *New York Times,* August 30, 1991. Retrieved November 12, 2007 (http://query.nytimes.com/gst/fullpage.html?res = 9D0CEFDA1131F933A0575BC0A967958260).

Colford, Joseph E., Ph.D. "Sports Participation for Children: A Parent's Guide." 1998. Retrieved November 11, 2007 (http://www.mciu.org/npintra/lib/npintra/mentalhealthfiles/sports_rk.html).

Court TV. "Self-Defense or Rage: Junta Trial Opens." 2002. Retrieved October 21, 2007 (http://www.courttv.com/trials/junta/010302_ctv.html).

Docheff, Dennis M., and James H. Conn. "It's No Longer a Spectator Sport: Eight Ways to Get Involved and Help Fight Parental Violence in Youth Sports." *Parks & Recreation,* Vol. 39, No. 3, March 2004, pp. 62–71.

ESPN. "Artest, Jackson Charge Palace Stands." 2004. Retrieved October 21, 2007 (http://sports.espn.go.com/nba/news/story?id = 1927380).

ESPN. "Harris Survey: X Games-Kids Favorite." 2000. Retrieved November 12, 2007 (http://www.espn.go.com/extreme/winterx00/s/jan26harrissurvey.html).

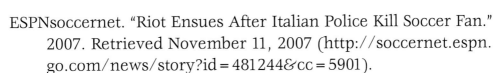

ESPNsoccernet. "Riot Ensues After Italian Police Kill Soccer Fan." 2007. Retrieved November 11, 2007 (http://soccernet.espn. go.com/news/story?id = 481244&cc = 5901).

Heinzmann, Gregg S. "Parental Violence in Youth Sports: Facts, Myth, and Videotape." *Parks & Recreation*, Vol. 37, No. 3, March 2002, pp. 66–77.

Hill, Jemele. "God's Quarterback Turning Everyone Into Believers." ESPN, 2007. Retrieved November 9, 2007 (http://sports.espn.go.com/espn/page2/story?page = hill/ 071107&sportCat = nfl).

Jordan, Pat. "A Family Tragedy in the Name of Love. (Tennis Player Mary Pierce's Family)." 1993. Retrieved November 12, 2007 (http://www.encyclopedia.com/ doc/1G1-14655941.html).

Lambert, Craig A. "The Dow of Professional Sports." *Harvard Magazine*, 2001. Retrieved October 21, 2007 (http://harvardmagazine.com/2001/09/the-dow-of-professional.html).

Layden, Tim. "The Big Hit." *Sports Illustrated*, Vol. 107, No. 4, July 30, 2007, p. 52.

Leonard, Wilbert. *A Sociological Perspective of Sport*. Minneapolis, MN: Burgess, 1984.

Library of Congress. "The Business of Professional Football." 2005. Retrieved October 21, 2007 (http://www.loc.gov/rr/business/ BERA/issue3/football.html).

MacDonald, G. Jeffrey. "After the Big Game, Why Is There a Riot Going On?" *USA Today*, November 1, 2004, p. 06D.

Mannix, Daniel P. *The Way of the Gladiator*. New York, NY: ibooks, inc., 2001.

Margolis, Jeffrey A. *Violence in Sports: Victory at What Price?* Berkeley Heights, NJ: Enslow, 1999.

Murphy, Shane. *The Cheers and the Tears: A Healthy Alternative to the Dark Side of Youth Sports Today.* San Francisco, CA: Jossey-Bass, 1999.

National Sporting Goods Association. "2006 Participation—Ranked by Total Participation." 2007. Retrieved November 11, 2007 (http://www.nsga.org/public/pages/index.cfm?pageid=150).

Nevius, C. W. "Soccer Players Get the Silent Treatment—and It's a Good Thing." SFGate.com, October 15, 2004. Retrieved November 12, 2007 (http://www.sfgate.com/cgi-bin/article.cgi?f=/c/a/2004/10/15/EBG6N959LP1.DTL).

New York Times. "Pierce to Drop Father as Coach." July 22, 1993. Retrieved November 12, 2007 (http://query.nytimes.com/gst/fullpage.html?res=9F0CE7DA1631F931A15754C0A965958260).

New York Times. "Pierce to Seek Court Order on Father." July 28, 1993. Retrieved November 12, 2007 (http://query.nytimes.com/gst/fullpage.html?res=9F0CE5DC1230F93BA15754C0A965958260).

Nichols, Rachel. "Remembering the Brawl." ESPN, 2005. Retrieved October 21, 2007 (http://proxy.espn.go.com/nba/news/story?id=2226703).

Phil Adams Athletic Scholarship Concierge Service. "Athletic Scholarships." 2007. Retrieved November 11, 2007 (http://www.philadamsportsrecruiting.com).

Phillips, Roger, and Michael Sudhalter. "Violence Increasingly Part of Youth Sports: Brawls, Assaults, Even Deaths Part of Troubling Unsportsmanlike Trend." *Stockton Record,* February 4, 2007. Retrieved November 21, 2007 (http://www.positivecoach.org/SubContent.aspx?id=1720).

Reiss, Mike. "Keeping Score Isn't Goal—or Is It?" Boston.com, 2006. Retrieved November 12, 2007 (http://www.boston. com/news/local/articles/2006/06/05/keeping_score_is nt_goal____or_is_it).

Sens, Josh. "How to Raise a Tour Pro." *Golf Magazine*, Vol. 47, No. 10, October 2007, p. 92.

State of New Jersey. "New Jersey's Code of Conduct Law." Rutgers Youth Sports Research Council, 2002. Retrieved November 12, 2007 (http://youthsports.rutgers.edu/ resources/legal-1/new-jerseys-code-of-conduct-law).

USA Today. "Brawl Timeline." 2005. Retrieved October 21, 2007 (http://www.usatoday.com/sports/basketball/nba/2004-11-21-brawl-timeline_x.htm).

USA Today. "Ugly Sports Incidents Nothing New." November 20, 2004. Retrieved October 21, 2007 (http://www.usatoday. com/sports/2004-11-20-sports-incidents_x.htm).

Wagner, Chris. "Pressure Points." YouthMinistry.com, 2007. Retrieved November 11, 2007 (http://www.youthministry. com/?q = node/4819).

INDEX

About the Author

Brian Wingate is an author, father, and sports fan with twenty years' experience in organized youth sports. A graduate of the University of North Carolina at Chapel Hill, Brian holds a B.A. degree in sociocultural anthropology. He is the author of several nonfiction books for young adults on sports topics. The American Library Association selected his biography of Tony Hawk as a Quick Pick for readers ages twelve to eighteen.

Photo Credits

Cover (left) © www.istockphoto.com/Ed Hidden; cover (center), pp. 23, 25 © AP Photos; cover (background) and back cover © www.istockphoto.com/Scott Leigh; p. 1 © www.istockphoto.com; p. 4 © NBAE/Getty Images; pp. 9, 37, 41 © Getty Images; p. 11 © HIP/Art Resource, N.Y.; p. 14 © Louis Deluca/Dallas Morning News/Corbis; p. 17 © AFP/Getty Images; p. 19 © Scott Wachter/Icon Sports Media; p. 21 © Bakersfield Californian; p. 27 © Thad Parsons/Icon Sports Media; pp. 30, 44 © Dennis MacDonald/Photo Edit; pp. 32, 46, 49 © David Young-Wolff/Photo Edit; p. 34 © Wade Jackson/Icon Sports Media; p. 38 © Bettmann/Corbis; p. 43 © Matt Lutton/Icon Sports Media; p. 52 © Tony Donaldson/Icon Sports Media.

Designer: Nelson Sá; **Editor:** Christopher Roberts
Photo Researcher: Marty Levick